Some Words Never Sleep

Zinia Mitra

Indie Blu(e) Publishing
Havertown, Pennsylvania

PRAISE FOR *SOME WORDS NEVER SLEEP*

"Zinia Mitra's poems record each lived moment's limitlessness where everything is, lives and breathes or just ceases to be unnoticed. For her, silences have their own modes of prayer. Time and again; asking is giving, Zinia responds to the very special intimacies including a sapling's delayed growth through space and time."

—Jaydeep Sarangi, a fellow contemporary poet and academic anchored in Kolkata/Jhargram.

"Zinia Mitra is a poet, feminist, honourable agent-provocatuer, and game-changer. Each poem in her new collection speaks to the challenges and opportunities of our times. Without denying difficulties, Mitra's words give us hope. These poems signal the challenges, but also, the way forward. The language is precise, the imagery striking. This book echoes with presence and dreams towards better futures. It must be read."

—Dr Amelia Walker, published poet and lecturer in creative writing on Kaurna Land, aka the Adelaide Plains, at the University of South Australia.

Some Words Never Sleep
Zinia Mitra, 2021
All rights reserved.

Printed in the United States of America.

No part of this book may be used, stored in a system retrieval system, or transmitted, in any form or in any means by electronic, mechanical, photocopying, recording or reproduced in any manner whatsoever without written permission from the publisher, except in the case of brief quotations embodied in critical articles and reviews.

For information, address
Indie Blu(e) Publishing
indieblucollective@gmail.com

ISBN: 978-1-951724-10-8 Print
ISBN: 978-1-951724-11-5 Digital
Library of Congress Control Number: 2021945319
Edited by: Candice Louisa Daquin
Cover Illustration & Interior Artwork: Lakshmi Tara
Cover Design: Christine E. Ray

ACKNOWLEDGEMENTS

My heartfelt thanks to the editorial team at Indie Blu(e) Publishing, especially Candice Louisa Daquin, editor of this volume.

My thanks to Lakshmi Tara for the stunning cover illustration and for her intuitive artwork based on the poems.

PREFACE

I am exuberant when someone addresses me as a poet. For all the criticisms that poets have to face, it is still a term that qualifies one for a special imaginative power. By the term 'poet', I mean and include, all those who have composed poetry, have scribed them, and also those who have never written them down. I was that kind of poet myself. I put down my first words on a page after years of writing poetry in my mind. It is a challenge to write the words down that float in. Sometimes, I do not want to surrender to them. For words are never quite equivalent to our emotions, never exactly equivalent to our experience.

There is a constant slippage between the self and the world and between the self and others– it sometimes pushes the corners of the self into an awareness inside the body that looks around at the world and impulsively tries to express all that it sees and feels through the words available. Emotions give birth to poetry. Discipline structures them. But poetry inevitably takes us into a visionary world, opens another door, even when it records only the concrete realities happening around us. Words woven into poetry may carry different connotations than those suggested by their controlled lexical meanings. These metaphorical meanings sometimes strike the mind before the decoding mechanism unfolds. Poetry, thus, exists between individual perception and the wakeful logical understanding of the mind. Every poetry collection is an addition to the ever-growing rhizome to which we all respond to unconsciously. That is why, I think, some images arise so easily, appear so familiar to us, while others are deeply personal images, closed images, and are difficult to comprehend. Poetry offers another sky, an emotive landscape. Poetry was always there with me. Poetry will always be there with me, even when I do not write it down. It is the true *flaneur* of life and mind.

I have been writing poetry for a long time. This collection is an effort, at the request of my poet friends, especially, Jaydeep Sarangi, the bilingual poet, to bring together my poems that have been published in various magazines and journals into a single volume. In the process, I wrote several new poems. Some of the poems here are new and appear *only* in this volume. Some of the poems in this collection were written over decades and are now selected and collected together for the first time.

I will remain ever obliged to my friends who have inspired me to undertake this journey.

Zinia Mitra

FOREWORD

When poems have the power to transport the reader through a steady rhythm on a promising track, the lines are lifted off the page and images assert a winged capability. Reading the 45 poems in Zinia Mitra's first collection, *Some Words Never Sleep* brings home this propelling quality of verse. Though the collection is prefaced with lines from Margaret Atwood's "Owl Song" in which the overpowering singularity of a death song is evoked, the poems here pulsate with living hues, cascading memories of tangible life, a sustaining landscape, a populous urbanscape, interwoven with women's voices– familial (Thammi, her Grandmother), literary (Sylvia Plath), legendary (Shakuntala) or social– the ubiquitous, universal mother – made audible by Zinia's own feminine consciousness.

Zinia's poems are rooted locally as she turns 'slowly into earth.' The reader is taken to the land watered by the Teesta, which carries within its flow the 'warmth of ravines and gorges... the warm smell of tropical deciduous trees', a river which the poet urges to flow to 'you' and it does, bringing with it the green aura of pine trees in the Darjeeling Himalayas. In her poetry, she knocks on the door of North East Indian Poetry, suggestive of a geographical proximity.

For me, Zinia's poetry is like a homecoming, as are the places she evokes, the Oxford Bookstore in Darjeeling, the Sukna forest slopes on the foothills of North Bengal, the beckoning necklace of lights of Tindharia town on the Himalayan heights or the neat rows of tea bushes in gardens where two leaves and a bud are plucked by 'tired native hand' to be savoured in white porcelain cups by people living comfortable lives. There is a note of compassion here which trembles on the edges of our consciousness.

This compassion can be laden with a sense of social injustice recognizing 'Hunger burns in the poor, like fire/ Desire burns in the rich, like fire'. And tied to compassion, is anger for the sizzled woman who might rebel in time, anger expressed in the kitchen, 'boiling/boiling' with domestic abuse finding expression in 'the whining cry of a child/hit against the walls', a chilling reminder of the price paid for an 'unpaid dowry.' Hers is a voice that augments the stream of Indian women poets writing in English, begun by Toru Dutt and Sarojini Naidu and continuing today.

There is a pervasive wind of fear blowing through the portrayed daily lives, with an absent father returning intermittently, the violence on defenseless lives during inebriated nights. The wail of a child who pleads, 'Let me in/now that father is dead' has the sharp clarity of ekebana, where the shadow cast by trimmed branches of too many details which can be gleaned from the images that conjure years of abuse, of beatings, the suffering inflicted on generations of women, culminating in a child's unshakable terror.

The pent-up emotions can be cleansed by rain as windows are opened to 'let the raining hours in', or drenched by monsoons and by the 'language of flowers', in the certainty of their seasonal beauty, the '*shiuli – palash – akondo*' or the '*nagkeshar*'. These flowers have the associative tenderness of '*Thammi*', the assuring presence in poems where the grandmother's poems merge with the granddaughters, as words flow through the generations, 'an ancient language. . . gathered' from her 'green notebook' which blend, dissolving differences between 'yours and mine'.

All through this collection there is evidence of the joy of playing with and taming words, juggling multiple languages that mark the Indian polyglot reality. My favourite is the hint of a mixed metaphor in spices and taste recalled from the 'spontaneity of childhood', of unripe mango pieces slashed with the sharpness of 'mustard paste/ sprinkled with salt and sugar and green chili choice cuts.'

This is the variety that makes this debut collection a delectable feast– of tastes, colours, emotions, passions, themes and scenes. And flowing through the volume is the Teesta river. For the poet, her 'river flows lonely', but beneath the overpowering current, one hears a voice that lags behind, asserting that it is

'Always alone' as 'Every journey is a lone one.' In actuality, this is not what stays with the reader. What remains is the memory of 'The Baul Singer who took his Leave,' but whose rhythms continue to haunt the reader's consciousness like the train that transports us to a timeless realm where 'dates' slip by and the moment is prolonged for us in poetry, poetry that is changeable but constant like the moon and its moods, like 'a woman's body/Dancing across the timeline of the sky.'

Zinia's collection *Some Words Never Sleep* asserts a discernible poetic voice that defies death as it affirms life on earth. Zinia endorses a thriving culture of Indian Poetry in English that is distinctively rooted in the local, with a global appeal.

Bashabi Fraser, CBE
Professor Emerita of English and Creative Writing
Director, Scottish Centre of Tagore Studies (ScoTs)
Edinburgh Napier University

TABLE OF CONTENTS

Earth	1
The Trees are Buddhas	3
Lag	5
The many deaths	7
Our Languages	9
On reading her story	11
Inflammable	13
Anger	15
Darjeeling	16
Teesta I	17
Teesta II	19
Tea	21
When the blessing is done	22
All this happened a while ago	24
Bouquet of Hyacinths	26
The Wail	28
Love	30
Sorrows	32
I met an old poet	33
Marigolds	35
The Clouds	37

When it Rains	39
This Rain	42
Charak	43
The Baul Singer who took his Leave	44
The Flower	46
Thoughts	48
Shadow Prison	49
Long-stalked Yellow Flower	51
Places	53
Poems	54
Pieces	56
COVID Lockdown/22nd March 2020	57
Lockdown Again	59
Amphan	60
Every journey is a lone one	61
Not You Alone	63
Essences	64
Monsoon	65
The Birds	66
Tonight	69
Spring	70
Guilt	72

Days	74
Some Words Never Sleep	75

I sit in the forest talking of death
Which is monotonous:
Though there are many ways of dying
There is only one death song...
—*Owl Song*, Margaret Atwood

Zinia Mitra

Earth

As I slowly turn into the earth
I perceive my gnarled roots have gone deep down
like that of a two hundred year-old banyan tree
with dark green symmetrical tangled leaves
and tenacious vines, some of which crawl into the
dark recess of the earth
to form other hungry roots. As I slowly turn into the earth
I perceive that I hold quiet water
in my palms, water from stagnant ponds
and green freshwater lakes. Also, ancient teardrops
from mourning eyes.
Before turning into the earth, I discern
that the lid of the dense blue sky is open
the planar clouds' meaningless forms
play shapes of fearful animals
hulking bears and sharp-tooth alligators
float about like old scars.
Then there are no more shapes to play.
Then it rains to create another sapphire space.

As I slowly turn into earth, I perceive that
I think of your green rimmed eyes. Sometimes.

Some Words Never Sleep

The Trees are Buddhas

The trees are Buddhas.
They stand rapt in intense
meditations together and make forests.
When the melancholic winds break against their feet
they preach peace. They shed their memories
like autumnal leaves.

Born on the moist earth
the trees bloom fragrant flowers
like love. Greener leaves sprout like sutras in Spring
to whisper truths.

The seasons dance their melodies on the boughs
adorn them with new leaves, new fruits
then strip them away.
The trees then live the furrowed barks
and yellowed leaves. Ripe seedy fruits fall on the earth
each seed is wooed to grow a tree. Spring arrives to fulfill them.
The trees grow old secretly after every Spring
they draw coded rings deep inside their trunks
and wither away. Preachers of deep silence they live
the rhythm of the cosmos.

We die many times in our lifetime like the trees
are renewed with every Spring that comes our way

and after a season of fruits and flowers' burden
carrying our own floral memories
we die.

Gust rolls the fallen leaves
across forest floors. Bamboo flutes
make somber music.
The tall green trees silently embrace the seasons.

We all are undeciphered rings in the end.

Zinia Mitra

Lag

Lag is failure to keep up with others
in a movement or a development;
a period of time between one event and another;
a retardation in an electric current flow;
also, another term for strings*
-strings tie up
our bits and pieces when we lag behind.
It is a harrowing feeling of exclusion
like a torn scrunched page that lands outside the bin
or like the silence of hours when a companion has
hired a sturdy boat
and left the curved shores of life
and we grow conscious of the dead wet sand under
our feet
and question the meaninglessness of the oblong
bubbles of water that pop up.

Sometimes it is pleasant to lag behind
when all the others with their backpacks have
hurried away
to look at the crumpled bed sheets
used towels and lipstick- stained coffee cups
to imagine their very, very busy sunlit days.

Sometimes it is wonderful to lag behind
in a relationship where the other has moved away

Some Words Never Sleep

listen to old songs, feel the dog- eared books, smile at the photographs
and imagine the fresh tapering fingers of friendship holding his hand.

Sometimes I lag behind to savor these fine moments to know that I exist. Always alone.

*North American billiards

Definitions from Oxford Languages

The many deaths

Sometimes it feels like death
not a cosmic death in a starry sky
but suffocating diurnal hours of closed windows.
Death is not a Keatsian reaper
resting briefly on a bright yellowish- green autumnal farmland
nor a Goghian harvester moving in broad daylight
flooded with golden light |
but a steel- gray thick fluid
falling falling falling like curtains of rain
on my closed glass windows. I am trapped
in between two worlds
in a glass square of obvious memories
and the submerged inconspicuous. Half- remembered
sentences- disjointed words- float in through the gap
under my heavy mahogany door like rotten carcasses
of seahorses. Half- drowned names float in
like uprooted bleached corals. My yesterdays are
dead turtles.
I drift towards them sluggishly
then settle on the white ocean floor. A shoal
of somnolent aquatic creatures, swim around me.
Moss sticks on the edges of my eyelashes. A pain.
A memory of a pain

Some Words Never Sleep

prickles my furtive mind like dizzying life.
Animals nibble on my carcass past midnight.
I rise up
a bubble of a deep hurt. I surface to face
the loud tick of my nagging wall-clock
and the whirring whirring whirring of the ceiling fan
and the falling falling of the thick steel-gray fluid.
I wake up to another long reverie of a ruddy life,
open my windows
and let the raining hours in. Let it rain pain until
past midnight.

Our Languages

We speak too many languages
in a lifetime
as Indians we are all polyglots
we speak in other tongues cautiously
like picking bones out of fish
our mother tongue lives on and on in us
like Lata Mangeshkar's songs.

We speak the language of spontaneity in childhood
the language of rain dance
the language that smells of unripe mangoes
cut into small pieces mixed with mustard paste
sprinkled with salt and sugar and green chili choice
cuts,
when in love the language of love
through eyes and fingers
sometimes through our whole bodies
when out of love, the language of disgust
is an impatient movement of the hands.

As mothers we learn the language of prayers
holding our children close to our bosom
we pray for every child of every mother
for each tiny bud, yet to bloom.

Some Words Never Sleep

Rebellion is also a language
that leaves secret scars on the body.
Loneliness is a language
across the qwerty keyboard,
a language of the fingers.

Death is a language too.
Sometimes people choose it consciously
over their mother tongues.

Zinia Mitra

On reading her story

She stood at the crossroads of her life for him
she stood there liberated from the bondage of her everydayness.

He had asked her to leave her
                                      baggage behind
promised her that they would
                                      start afresh
that he would always be there
                                      for her
but she lugged the weight of
                                      moments
she couldn't leave behind.

All the raindrops on her leaves
all his poems they would read aloud
all the coffee bills they could laugh at
all her fresh ferns, spear grass,
train tickets and egret feathers,
a small water-bottle, some money
lipstick and comb,
also, memories of scratches on her dry barks
yellow leaves that had collected at her feet
in short, her bare essentials and a part of Sukna
Forest Range.

Some Words Never Sleep

She waited for him there
through all the droplets of water
that formed in the mouths of
the taps

                                        fell one by one

she waited for him there
until she was hungry and

                                        not hungry anymore

she waited for him there
until the last train

                                        left the platform

until the bodies around

                                        wrapped blankets

turned dead on the benches
until she was unburdened of

                                        all the tearing noises
                                        the world makes

until it was time to return home
until it was time to return home.

Inflammable

Is a woman gallant only if she can set the streets on fire?
They challenge her into conflagration,
like Ram did.
Sylvia Plath spelt out fire and sucked gasoline.
Mallika Sengupta set aflame Bangla words
that charred her skin.
Mary Wollstonecraft
displayed pain like jewelry
burned
and became gold.

One day she will stop stooping
the walls will collapse, the doe will sprint out
rejoice in the smell of wet leaves
wild woods
it will rain on her furrowed skin
after long years of cacti humiliations
and summers of sizzled flesh.
Meanwhile she collects her dry ribs
to set them on fire
the eyes of the doe waking through her bamboo leaves.
She displays her burn
like a tattoo, bleeding every day
not only once a month.
"It will clot with time," Mother says

cramming her wilderness into closeted memory.
She spreads out a colorful sari that she must wear.

They had judged her bones
her flesh, her hair
her facial expressions blurred out
like rape victims on TV.

Rape is everywhere
even of the mind
the hate performances that began in bed
stuffed her soul with carbonized cotton.

Yet she is the perfect host
but her smiles can fathom the gap between the signifier
and the signified.
The doe waits for her Shakuntala.

O Virginia!
had I room of my own
I would not walk the corridors with borrowed fire
maybe I could
have my own lexicon.

Anger

Tears moped the room
as the day slid in again and broke its back on the floor
her shadow broke away by turns
negotiating with the heaviness of her eyelids
heavy like breasts swelled with milk
the pains swam from one lake to another
soggy with questions
the answers were perhaps packed
in the empty bottles under her bed
adding up every night like personal blemishes.
Her body felt like squeezing of damp laundry
before it is hung out to dry.
Back in the kitchen she could not chop her inside
or roast the insults
just anger boiling
boiling
without ever reaching a point.
The sunless day felt so blue
like the color of her cheeks.
Her screams guarded her against fears
at night.
Night was a time when her cheeks turned red
somewhere the whining cry of a child
hit against the walls
heavy
like her hours of unpaid dowry.

Some Words Never Sleep

Darjeeling

Between creases of sleep and wakeful states of years
the molten sunlight flits on *ikshkus* leaves
eternity breathes behind the other slope
Darjeeling exists in a dream.

Pine trees shiver in green pherans
their aging shoulders stoop, touch mine
peace flags with Buddha's message
flap colorful undertones in the wind.

Kitchen fumes spiral upward
like affirmations of some hermetic faith
each footstep replies to the other in boulevard
silence
chor batos meander deep down into the
unconscious.

Memories swirl on teagarden gradients
yearning days, eager nights, dim yellow-bulbed love-
makings
cross the road to Oxford Bookstore
like the penumbra of a kite's full wingspan.

A whiff of horses' pungent smell
the gale eats into the flesh, rain.
I wrap a half-wet dream in my woolen shawl, scrawl
a name on a condensed windowpane.

Teesta I

Clouds hung solemn, like frowns of mythological gods
then it rained for eons drenching mountains
and green lives to the core
the alpine vegetation
the fairy green grass
or those that sprout strong and sharp, the turf
and when it finally stopped raining
Tao Lhamo Lake spread out her curly locks in the sun
it unfolded through landscapes we call
Rangpo, Kalimpong, Jalpaiguri, Mekhliganj
and traveled towards the land we call Bangladesh
carrying the indigo blue sky in her bosom
carrying the warmth of ravines and gorges
the warm smell of tropical deciduous trees
the alpine vegetation, the verdure
the music of women filling their pitchers
the rhythm of women walking down her rocky shores
the laughter of children playing on her banks
and the quietness of the fallen sal leaves.

Some Words Never Sleep

Teesta II

Teesta is the eye of my land
it links the green land to the blue sky
all that flies in the air
all the structures that stand on the land
angular, spherical, hollow,
or rise in the mind like the lax cottony molds
undulate in her, breaking and joining and breaking again
on the reflected sapphire of the sky.

My river flows towards you.

Teesta is the life of my land
like my veins it carries the pulsation
through rows of overpopulated slums
with dingy shops that play loud music
between the sentient sal trees' silent communication
between quantize boulders, mossy rocks and warm turf.
Men and women here are tied to her with a string.

My river carries their memory.

When rhododendrons rattle off their red
pine trees drop their cones, or pungent fruits
from fruit trees fall and break
droning her sibilant, rehearsing her song, she flows

Some Words Never Sleep

for it is music that separates her waters from the supple land
from the emotions of a forest that had bloomed beside the wrinkled riverbed of your eyes.

My river flows lonely.

Tea

I watch their hands pluck the two green eyes
of Buddha
their heads silently accede
earth in their nails smell of sweet potatoes.
Soft cloths folded into baskets
hang from their heads like white clouds
green leaves fall on green leaves.
An afternoon of heaviness.
Bees fly to their hives
a brain fever bird calls.

The sun sets in the saucer landscape
the mountains lose their white

rows of muddy bare feet
communicate with ancient roots.
The smell of a mud-coated boiling pot
black leaves swim in the boiling water
like tadpoles
then settle down
white teacups like miniature landscapes
hold the sacred infusion.
A tired native hand closes the red sun
I hear her footsteps closing in my head.

When the blessing is done

Goddess Kali
stands beside the paddy field
alone. The exposed clay bulges
were once her breasts.
The weather has stolen
many of her skulls,
a few still hang there
beneath her navel.
Only some hands
in her girdle stick faithful
to cover her shame.

The family has prospered they say
after the puja
done so fervently.
The paddy can now proficiently hide
the remnants of Shiva at her feet.

The puja was done meticulously, they say.
The women of the house
saw to it that the fruits were sliced right
before the offering,
that the *bael* leaves were washed and arranged.
The incense sticks gave out
an overpowering jasmine scent.

Zinia Mitra

The *khichri* carried the smell of *ghee*, they say,
marigold petals had to be picked out
of *chutney* too.

An outline of a female figure
stands watching the western sky
where the sun turns dull late afternoon
then crouches behind the shapeless trees.
Twilight dawns on a lonely paddy field
mingling the discarded blue with inky blackness.
A kingfisher bird warbles on an electric pole
clad in the same hue.

All this happened a while ago

All this happened a while ago ...
a verdant lawn, a swing
a frail nervous girl standing at the verge of
a swing-full of dreams
hesitant to climb
under the watchful eyes of her mother
somewhere a threat
a lurking fear of her father.
The everyday pretenses at games
the stamping and running on green naked grass
the weekly pretenses at friendship
the hugs, the gifts, the gift-wrappers, meaningless cards,
the evening pretenses at studies
digging dreams out of the holes in the syllabus.
Then the pretense of growing up
quietly watching the rebellious body
tremble like fronds in monsoon
each pinna unfolding in the warmth of the sun
the pretenses of interests in aunties gossip
falling loudly like tear shaped raindrops on glass windows
the secrets of suppressed yawns
hanging clouds of sleep on eyelids.
Then the pretense of household
the clatters, the clinks, the clangor
the game of shadows on the walls.

Zinia Mitra

The shadows grew taller.
The shadows came nearer
almost suffocating her then moved away.
All this happened a while ago ...

Now she and her oblique shadow
are free to oscillate on the surface of her swing-dreams
play games on the expansive lawn
fall across the swing or onto the green grass
or choose not to fall at all.

Bouquet of Hyacinths

grandma's photo frame
black limits to a monochrome world.

Branches outside my window
survive through seasons
bend and imitate
ibis, sometimes
egret's long neck.

Starlit sky slithers into my room
scattering secrets
in hushed impassivity.

Grandma collected her secrets
like a shell collector
along the banks of Ganga
from the cracked steps
that went down into the unfathomable river
sometimes on country boats in breaking sunlight
where the oars broke up time into a series of dreams
a bouquet of hyacinths floated on her gandhian
spectacles.

I walk on the terrace to pluck a white quill
from the tree that has survived the seasons
playing ibis and sometimes the egret's long neck.
Grandma had a white quill with a blemish of ink

that unabashedly revealed her memories
pages preserved with discolored neem leaves
distorted partially by time.

The Wail

Let me in
now that father is dead
I am still that frightened child
peeping through the gap
under your closed door
my cheeks touching your lifeless floor.
I was scared of father
of his size (he was wise)
his black -framed square glasses,
his seriousness, his official files
that allowed no mistakes anywhere,
I played with flies; my page full of mistakes
was flung outside your closed door.
There would be a lot of rustle, cooker whistle
in the kitchen, cuttings and beatings and frying
when he was home.
I was the quiet, sneaking child
roaming in the kitchen garden
waiting for father to go. I was slow.
I was scared of father
of his loud voice
his loud alcoholic friends
and when you whined and complained about me
of his abuses, of the cold floor
outside your closed door.
The lone hours of watching the moon
stiff from my bed pretending sleep

kept me awake for nights
and I could hear grandma's wails
see her frights
see her lost daughter shine in the moonlight
a mist- pale- pale and white.
Her tears like fairies with wings
escaped the house playing flutes
there were noise of boots
as father's alcoholic friends left the house.
You drowsed in your siesta
while grandma and myself collected *dumur*
from the forest nearby that smelled of *nagkesar*
dumur that you so liked to cook
but the look that you gave me, the look
stayed with me for years
whether I made love or war.
I did none of the things you thought I did
I was an obedient kid
but you whined and complained
and I hid
I was a ghost, most-ly
but now that father is dead
your footsteps unsure and lean
let me in.

Some Words Never Sleep

Love

I want to connect
the spaces left by your songs
before the light changes forever on Tindharia Hills.
Something grew heavy in my throat those days
looking over the monotonous gradient, talking of
waking mountains
like the soggy drooping of dark green pine-leaves.
Something grew light in my feet, those days
like I could sprint across the Sukna forest slope
like I could leap up to touch the evening star
a trembling flow inside me like a canopied rivulet
every time your eyes touched mine
a green solitude.

I want to connect
the spaces left by your touch
the old road, the bench, the trunk of the tree.
Something grew definite in my eyes those days
when my skin dissolved under your words
and my eyes held out their hands to you.

Floating above the wary fence I choose this
figurative life
because love sometimes grows too heavy
like the idea of God
to carry literally.

Some Words Never Sleep

Sorrows

Thammi asked me to pinch up her sorrows
like red ants from the bark of her tree
they climbed her long brown arms
one by one from imprisoned nights
when saltwater overflowed her pores
and the rain disoriented the shape of the girl
who always floated above her, trapped in a form.
In her dreams she had kept her young.

I reached out across many years to touch her hands
her dry skin peeled off
a strong cinnamon smell persisted in my fingers.
Memories of spices wafted through the air
like flipped pages of her torn recipe books
basmati rice, ghee, saffron, cardamom,
milk and honey dripping from their dog- eared
edges.

I boil a glass of clove water
white puffy clouds form around the semicolon moon
outside
my fingers adamantly repeat the cinnamon smell
memory of her dry skin.

Zinia Mitra

I met an old poet

I met an old poet.
She was groping her way through her memories
when we knocked against each other.
She spoke in archaic language
her words opened
like wooden doors on creaking hinges
swollen by a season of rain
some words a thunder
across my sky
her images blinded me like lightning.

We walked the empty auditorium
across the rain-washed lawn
she wanted to go to the river.
We passed the fish market
where words were weighed and cut into pieces
we passed a library where words were preserved
in book folds
read and whispered.

Her words, inundated with memories,
smelled like old books
wild love in their pages
wild flowers
where a thousand butterflies flapped their wings
in bright sunlight.

Some Words Never Sleep

Broken relationships are torn pages of manuscripts
the ink dilutes in the rain
and the words break, then dissolve in water.
Clouds speak in raindrops like the plants speak in flowers.

Raindrops fell from the sky onto our umbrella
and scattered around us
on the grass
like her words
each a small world of the poet and her reader.

Marigolds

"Marigold, marigold!"
Your voice drowns the Winter tales of Tindharia
hills.
"Get me a marigold."
I wrap myself in a coarse hand-woven Bhutanese
shawl
and walk the earthy lanes of the dark green tea
garden
as your silence falls
outside Winter's windows
like frilled black shadows of the rows of pine trees
that always stand there in the horizon.
The winter fog stretches over our tea garden.
The illusion of your voice drowns in the loud noise
of waterfalls.
I look for marigolds on the scarfs of winter
in the womb of mountains
trail their strong smell on the silvery hairs of tea
leaves
throughout my blurred elliptical days.

They are migratory birds
fleeting from one hill to another
with cryptic seeds in their beaks
surprising the eye of the Winter sun
with sudden bloom in unforeseen places.

Some Words Never Sleep

They perorate their Winter tales
on grassy gradual
on jagged imperceptible slopes. The Marigolds.

The Clouds

We can halt only at the halt-stations.
Whenever you and I go out for a walk, it rains.
A jumble of half formed- thoughts beyond
the hanging bridge
look for shelter.

There is a coffee shop close by
frequented by travelers like you
who traveled the world never in the realms of gold
but in the domains of lead-heavy reality
witnessing hunger and riot and death
for reasons such as food habits and God
both of which you never understand.
Food is that which fills a hungry stomach
and Gods never ask for blood, you say.
You never understand the ways of our Gods
who sit at road corners vermillion -smeared, of our
Gods
who lurk in the fears and the dark desires of men
asking money for blessings and also sacrifices.
God is like the river, you say
and drink deep into my eyes.
God is fulfillment, you say,
and food is that which fills an empty stomach.
Not a morsel is wasted here, you say
every modicum is food for someone.
I look at the trees rejoicing in the rain

Some Words Never Sleep

every leaf turning greener
the earth drinking in every drop
quivers like a sophisticated lady.
I cross the bridge with you and walk into
the coffee shop. The clouds
of my mind rain into the river.

When it Rains

We were waiting undefined
squatting on mud floors
leaning against haystacks
or hanging onto the rods in crowded buses,
when it rained.

It rained on paddy fields
like a well-rehearsed dance drama
like Tagore's poems read aloud
it spread a palliative across traffic,
acrimony, remorse and regret.

Black umbrellas danced
on glossy black roads
meandering in from the past.
It also rained on the roads
I never walked alone.

It had been a season of bare branches
yellow grass and quiet toads.
A season of earthen pitcher-water
and hand-fans in irate hands.

When it rains, one tracks
the dream-clouds covertly preserved,
in the northeast corner of the mind,
inhales in the dance drama

Some Words Never Sleep

the lost rhythm of youth.

Black umbrellas push into puny tea-shops
a crowd of sweating people
sit on wooden benches
holding fuming tea cups
accumulating vapors in their minds.

Zinia Mitra

This Rain

No one has written about this rain,
this rain that drenched me
this rain that walked in uninvited, into my lost-umbrella day
drowned the emerald grass, succulent leaves and furrowed barks
no one has written about these fine gray lines
that trembled at the edge of this autumnal storm
like silver hairs on an aging face,
the hushed approval, of the last ardent sunrays
the breathless moments before the rain
when the world suspended itself and hung from the sky.
I have collected these transient moments
because I want to write about this rain.

We all can feel the lightning that strikes our trees in distant lands.

Charak

A calendar year changes its side
I can feel the hours creak around their hinges.
The year turns
like the *charak* tree
slowly at first
then faster and faster, till we feel giddy.
A dark woman pulls me by the hand
takes me right under the tree;
Look. I see my representative
hang upside down, by a hook above the fire.

Hunger burns in the poor, like fire
Desire burns in the rich, like fire
Thoughts burn in desire, like fire
the mind churns.
Corpses burn in fire and turn into ash.
Lash
A boy lashes himself
then extends his begging bowl
the yellow hungers around his eyes lash me.

Some Words Never Sleep

The Baul Singer who took his Leave

The tree ripped itself
and oozed out a thousand, blood–red *palash* flowers
like open wounds.
The unsteady, gyrating wind picked up
an intimate red-dust-road scent. A solo *baul*
ambled along the road with his *ektara*

tomay hridmajhare rakhbo chere debo na*

The days that have taken their farewell are too
many!
Girls in yellow saris, with flowers around their buns
giggled and dawdled around the tree
searching for more colors.
It was then that he took his leave
like a poem ending too abruptly,
like a spectator anticipating
a too, too familiar ending
walks out of the opera house
muttering under his breath:
conventional, all too conventional!
Thus, he took his leave.
Madal- beats darted across the orchestra pit
and followed him down the staircase.
Kangira jhum –jhumed and rambled the streets
baul tunes hovered in the Spring air.
The yellow -saried girls tapped their feet

swayed and danced around the tree, in untamed
passion
until they slumped together with laughter,
their disheveled hair spread out on
the dusty ground, scattering flowers.
The tree stood still
oozing out a thousand, blood–red *palash* flowers.

*Translation: I will keep you within my mind and
never let you go.*

In memory of Kalikaprasad Bhattacharyya

The Flower

It is difficult to live like this
like the wheels of a huffing train
on the tracks of a time that is yours.
I occupy a secluded compartment.
I am a distant traveler on the train
patchwork of greenish - yellow paddy fields
shimmer outside my window
rivulets cut through my landscapes like couplets
bridges jingle aloud, breaking my monotonous
rhythm.
Who is driving this train?
Does he know why I undertake this journey
through your poetry across many years?
Was it too painful a death?
I know it is an art you were exceptionally well at.
I wish I could trim your pain like your hair
pull out your troubles
and kill them between my nails like lice,
oil your hair, make them tangle free
comb them until there was oil enough on my
fingertips
so much that I would be scared to turn the pages
of your poetry books.
Then I could carry the smell of your perfumed hair
in my fingers throughout my days.

Zinia Mitra

The fragrance of your poems
grows in me like spiky red flowers.
They call them Sylvias.

Thoughts

An unpainted multi-storied building
stands unaided, leaning against time
an unrealized colossal dream.
Its inmates have left for another country
their thoughts have remained back
trapped within this unrealized dream.
They reside in the rooms,
in kitchens, in washrooms,
in dining halls, in balconies
as thought forms without words, without expression,
like souls without bodies.
They look down through glass windows
into the streets where people whizz past each other
bodies bottled inside their thoughts.
An orphanage stands across the road
an open-armed Christ hangs on a cross with a drooping head.
A smile on his lips. The garden is open for orphan children to play.
Orphan thoughts reside unseen
in the house across the street, leaning against time.
The inmates have left for another country.

Shadow Prison

The traffic light switches from green to red
it stops all movement, briefly easing
the anguish of the souls playing at life.
It is a moment of release-
also of captivity,
a release from action
from illusion of action
but a confinement in time
and space.
The towering apartments around the traffic point
cast their gloomy, jagged shadows on the streets
to construct a shadow prison.
Ombromanie.
Men and women of this city
disparate karmic strings and footsteps
has brought them here, this moment,
their orbits have crossed abruptly.
There is nothing abrupt here. No accidents.
We are all trapped here in this laconic prison.
Shadow prisoners wait for movement.
It grows hot and sultry,
only the umbra of low flying crows
glide across the square noiselessly
like dusky floating clouds. A paper kite
trapped in a cable wire imitate their flights.
Two pigeons in grey coats
pace up and down a parapet wall

studying the inmates grimly.
Prison walls grow taller, as the sun
takes a step towards the west. The walls will
altogether disappear
with sunset. Anxiety mounts as impatient inmates
yearn to break away from this shadow prison house
that confines them now. Motionless
breathing shallow, we wait for the light to go green
like we always wait to escape illusions.

Long-stalked yellow Flower

Should we be glad, we lived the moment-
the moment of your picking a long- stalked yellow flower
and clipping it on my longish brown hair? You said
you wanted to collect all the yellow flowers
that grow on Tindharia slopes, throughout your sunburnt days
bring them to me on a long island moonlit night
hold my hands, till the sun cleared your gray, convex horizon—
it was such a limpid dance of words!
Later, the coded bar suffocated me, with steamed fish,
the partying men and women, wrapped me in loneliness.
I am no Mrs. Dalloway. I hate the clinking of glasses.

In a sense, we are all Clarissas
absurd perhaps in the eyes of our own Peters
organizing our grand parties
with words and thoughts and ideas
that eat and drink and dance and blather
throughout our lives.

Some Words Never Sleep

Our lives are like scratches made by wolves' claws
on the surface of our wet- soil minds
scratches on bare skins, when we stand naked,
dripping water
tiny points of ache, forming on our old scars.

We greet our scars like familiar kitchen containers
look for them in the throng of voluble memories
feel at home with chopping on the chopping board.
Much of it, is inside.

Places

I could never reach
the place I
wanted to. *The Lonely Planet* guide
left me searching
for the right one beyond
the meandering roads where
at every turning, a God
scrutinized me.
All my mistaken
destinations had their
pine forests that dropped cones
on the roads, all forests had their
singing birds. Songs that
blend with the flow of Teesta
have always held me
in trance, especially
the songs concerning sad pasts.
All pasts are somewhat sad, like all
pine forests that slope
downwards
towards darkness.

Poems

You spoke in an ancient language
your words opened up
like walnuts.

I gathered them
broke them open
the inside was a brain.

I ate the brains
I ate your words.

Thammi, your laughter was like a saw
that cut into my unseasoned wooden planks.
Our legs buried deep in the mud
we waded the waters before we climbed the boat
you and me.
You sang aloud the many rhymes you composed
taught me the language of flowers
shiuli –palash –akondo
You taught me how to sow seeds in the dust
chase wild crabs to find their homes
collect *nagkeshar* from beneath the huge tree
behind the shadowed post office.
I left you there alone under the mythical tree
I still feel the pain like a sharp stab.

You will be in my eternity.
Your words
from your green notebook
split open
the poems melt into each other
then with mine
to make one volume of poems
yours and mine.

Pieces

Perhaps I had looked at the light for too long
when I shut my eyes, the memory of it hovered
inside me
lit my inside
like the inside of the refrigerator lights up
when we open its doors
and makes visible, the dead plants,
the pieces of dead fish that we preserve.
A rotten smell hangs in the air
someone sweeping a littered backyard
the stink of dead fish attracts flies
who soar and make rounds like stray thoughts
before their final dismissal.

The dead fish will wait here in silence
for someone else to open the door
to pick up the scent and let the flies hover again.

I collect my broken ribs
scattered throughout the house
before it darkens.

COVID Lockdown/22nd March 2020

...then the ashen world paused its pace
childhood days awoke like childhood songs
from soft pillows of deep sleep
the languorous ways always
smell of wet grass.

The rain- washed streets
rest smooth like sandalwood paste
one or two vehicles pass
and when they pass
I can trail them like street dogs, till they are quite gone
green barbets briefly visit my hollow mind, then fly on.

Birds call out loud— *Ucopakhi, Dauk*
names resurface from childhood
I did not know they had hidden nests
in the holes our bodies had made.

Someone far is playing '*Musafir hoon yaro* ...'
a common household sparrow
hops across my empty hours
I can feel the beat
of its light dancing feet.

Some Words Never Sleep

Pigeons sit fluffed up in rows
their eyes closed; a crow sits quiet
my childhood in its eyes.

Pieces of memories tangled in my hair when freed
dances like the sparrow in the slow beat
Musafir hoon yaaro ...

Lockdown Again

the roads fold their ends
men are no more at work
speed limit sign boards
redundant

no mothers walk
their children to school in this dystopian world
no women on scooters take a quick look on the mirror
and rush to promised time slots

togetherness is a memory
that fades with every dropping sun
news of death and hunger
and hunger and death
and floating corpses in Ganga
shatter a tender generation
like shattered glass widows during the wars
we change rooms to hide our tears
turn off the news they shouldn't hear.

Caged birds wait for the dusk
a promise of homeward flight in their wings
the hushed world pauses beside
a blue river
waiting for sunrise.

Amphan

A page of a wet notebook is easily torn
like the mind
old aches lie scribbled on the leaves of trees
uprooted by the cyclone
a cosmos of events rewind on them.
Each of us had a window
that opened to a tree.
Each of us had a little sunshine, that brightened our days
like leaves after the rains.
When the branches of the uprooted trees were cut
after the storm to restore electric supply
the cries, the despairing cries
that we heard were ours
they were our pains that the trees had absorbed
along with our exhalations.

Some of us still have their leaves preserved in our old books.

Amphan was a cyclone that hit West Bengal on 16th May 2020.

Every journey is a lone one

Every journey is a lone one.
Men and women bent
with burdens
of past
of dreams
of memories
of ambitions
tread along the road
from different countries
the Planet Earth
showing each
a different destination
a different map route
different hotels with
different room rents.
If they speak to each other
even in the same tongue
they produce
Pinter's *Landscape*.

Our past is
another country
another city
its shabby houses do not
greet us well today

Some Words Never Sleep

yet we feel at home there
reconstructing lost furniture
and imaginary faces.

As children we all
looked up at the night sky for stars
unable to accept darkness as darkness
painted angels and Gods
painted houses
with Fathers and Mothers
husbands, wives and children
pretending to travel together
pretending to speak in the same tongue.
As elders
unable to accept darkness as darkness
we hide our distorted faces
behind our children's fabricated successes.

Not You Alone

Not you alone, here too
the moon rises with green pain
and stings my heart.
Here too, the days seem
endlessly wasted
the nights wrapped in typos.
Are you too, trying to hide a sob
in your road to endless compromise?
Here too, the moon throws sinister shadows
that disturbs my household.

Essences

When the moonlight fills me up spills over me
inhale me in. In your presence
I smell like the wood roses that fall
on dew topped night grass
I smell like the earth that soaks up the first monsoon
rainfall
when you take me into your fragranced rose garden
and we are alone
smell my pain. My pain
overpowers me like the sea
that breaks against an ancient rock but cannot
drown it.
Take my hand and smell it.
When you take me into your aroma suffused room
in the soft light, octave in your eyes, and we are
alone
smell my memories. In your presence
my memories smell like freshly plucked tea leaves
they smell like tea flowers that dance in the rain.
Take my hand.
Smell my pain.

Monsoon

The endless downpour finally swamps the soil
the night tiptoes through the rent in the clouds
like a beautiful girl stretches on the thatched roofs
in a soft cotton wrapped dream.
The wind plays melodies on her anklet
disturbs the dreamy dews on the cob
they tremble and fall on the earth, to be absorbed instantly.
Red berries fall and rot, water dribbles from the leaves.
Moist leaves spread a thick rug underneath.
Eddying in the water
swirls as it churns the memories
of our elders and their paper boats
that are feeble enough to drown in small apologetic waves
but strong enough to remain afloat
in river reminiscence.
The earth that eventually stole them of their childhood
turn black in our fingernails now
they carry the mephitic smell of aging and bags of moist sentiments on their back
the village of our elderly consciousness suffers monsoon.

The Birds

There are birds inside my head
they croon
through my long days
chirp chirp chirp.
I've never caught them silent
unlike the ducks that sit
contemplating their webbed feet
around that moss-grown pond
or float in the hushed waters that flower hyacinths

unlike the stout-billed sparrow
that preens its buffy-brown plumage silently

or unlike the kite's quiet hover
whose shadows glide across my terrace.

The birds sit on my crooked branches
peeving the silence that grows
around my ancient leaves
chirp chirp chirp.

A solitary *jarul* tree stands quiet
my sorrows bloom purple flowers
there must be birds' nests on her chiaroscuro
branches
for they sit long
meditative

Zinia Mitra

half- hidden from the mind's eye
screened by her dark green leaves
that open upwards towards the sky.
A pothos vine creeps up her thick trunk stealthily
all her giant leaves unfold earthwards
I have seen dry leaves at her feet
become sparrows and take flight.
A sfumato of *sal* trees
contour lines of a meadow
grows grass imperceptibly
the sun slides off the sky's back
and leaves the landscape
hushed up and sleepy.

All the noise is in the inside
chirp chirp chirp
croon the birds
through my long days
and waking nights.

Some Words Never Sleep

Tonight

The moon overwhelms me on your terrace tonight
I walk the length of the entire moon calendar
the waning moon
the crescent moon
the new moon,
the waxing moon
the gibbous moon
like the dance of a woman's body
across the timeline of the sky
until she is in full bloom, like tonight.
Breathless
intrepid
she watches us through your charcoal palm leaves.
Our shadows are like snakes coiling
twining
on a wet riverbed in moonlight
like your slithery leaved money plants
that grow around your empty hours, twirling their
dun vines
until you shed your old skin
and enter my full moon womb.
The moon is a woman's body
dancing across the timeline of the sky.

Spring

When Amzad Ali moved his fingers on his
sarod
my body oozed and turned my dress into
red
let us forget the other audience present
it was a semitone moment when
I bled.
That was my Spring.
It opened the eyes of the pollens in
my body
it blossomed my crooked branches
my petals
quivered, held quiet conversations
it quenched my deep blue thirst
with strong floral
wine.
I melted into the shades of that
fluid night
trembled in the shadows of tall sal trees,
rustling leaves,
a bird warbled a song somewhere
a squirrel scurried away with my Winter
forever
Spring broke suddenly on the rim of
my being.

Zinia Mitra

We all know that Spring is unstoppable
I responded like the river responds to
full moon.
*"What about the materiality of the body
Judy?"*
I needed to be restored to my bodily being
and all along I had thought that words
constructed us
it is Spring.

Guilt

I escape from the warmth of his segmented arms
open the car door
erase the imagined disquiet of the driver's eyes
peering in the rear-view mirror memory
and step outside into the cold freedom
carrying in my long- strapped leather bag
a purse, ATM cards
comb, lipsticks, hand cream, perfume
and the other things women usually carry,
the gerbera bouquet he gave me,
a floral printed scarf around my neck
nagging guilt hanging heavy from my other
shoulder.

Her dusky shadow had banged across my window
when our car paused at the crossing.
Her knock drowned out my song list
reminding me of the left-over cookies
partying children had refused to eat.

When the light changed
we took the fly over.
Her jaundiced eyes and hollow cheeks pursued me
on my Ola screen
throughout my long drive through the city.

Zinia Mitra

In the streets, these women are always there.
The brunette, the tan, the dark,
on pavements, engaged with their gaping cluttered households
surrounded by hungry children
their uncovered breasts hang like forgotten births.
They sleep on rugs in parks and on pavements
bang on car windows with begging bowls
sometimes carrying pictures of goddesses.
They are everywhere across the country
growing in the shadows of high-rises.

After long evenings of poetry or pianoforte
their shadows come alive.
They pursue me into Westside, Pantaloons, Global Desi, Madame
where lifeless mannequins are elaborately embellished
their pallid shadows accompany me into
restaurants, cafes, salons, book stores, sometimes
they flash smiles on cover pages.
They are everywhere. We have learned
to ignore them like morbid thoughts.

It feels increasingly heavy now
as if I have been cradling a hungry child for long hours
and need to shift the load.

Some Words Never Sleep

Days

Something has happened to the dates.
They are slipping by, without telling me
without letting me live inside them.
I lost a Wednesday the other day
and one Thursday, the week before.
You say days fly
they have golden wings and fly up to the sun
I wish their wax wings melt
I wish they fall down one, by one
day by day
their long and false tales, undo
their useless existence.

Some Words Never Sleep

some words never sleep

they enter the big mansions through holes at night
and watch in uneasy silence,

marvel at how they have erected strong walls
between inmates.
Some words hold each other by hands

close in barren worlds
create icy landscapes

with no flowers.
Sometimes words brush against each other to create
sparks

like pebbles on riverbanks
such sparks can light up our eyes and lips

long after the stones have been dropped.
Some words never sleep

they remain awake long after human eyes close
for the last time.

Some Words Never Sleep

"Earth" was originally published in *Poetry Potion*, 15th June 2020, and has been anthologized in *Poetry the Best of 2020: Poets of the World,* ed. Hülya N. Yılmaz, Professor Emerita, The Pennsylvania State University, Inner Child Press, 2021.

"The Trees are Buddhas" was originally in *Erothanatos: A Peer-Reviewed Quarterly Journal on Literature,* Vol. 4, Issue 3, September, 2020.

"On reading her Story" was originally published in *The Pangolin Review,* issue 13, November 18, 2019 and later anthologized in *The Kali Project: Invoking the Goddess Within,* eds. Candice Louisa Daquin and Megha Sood, Indie Blu(e) Publishing, 2021.

"Anger" was anthologized under the title "Tears" in *The Kali Project: Invoking the Goddess Within,* eds. Candice Louisa Daquin and Megha Sood, Indie Blu(e) Publishing, 2021.

"Darjeeling" was originally published in *Setu,* Pittsburgh, USA, June issue, 2020.

"Teesta I" was first originally in *Setu,* Pittsburgh, USA, June issue, 2019.

"Teesta II" was originally published in *Setu*, Pittsburgh, USA, June issue, 2019.

"Tea" was originally published in *TEXT Special Issue*, Number 60, *Indian-Australian exchanges through collaborative poetic inquiry*, October, 2020.

"When the blessing is done" was originally published in *Muse India*, Jan/Feb issue, 2011.

"The Wail" was first published in *Indian Literature* (Sahitya Akademi), issue 307, Sept-Oct 2018 and later anthologized in *The Kali Project: Invoking the Goddess Within*, eds. Candice Louisa Daquin and Megha Sood, Indie Blu(e)Publishing, 2021.

"Sorrows" was originally published in *The Antonym*, Feb 5 issue, 2021.

"The Clouds" was originally published *in Eastlit: Creative Writing, Literature and Art focused on East and South East Asia,* February issue, 2017.

"When it Rains" was first published in *Coldnoon: International Journal of Travel Writing and Travelling Cultures*, October issue, 2018.

"The Baul Singer who took his Leave" was originally published in *Muse India*, issue 74, July-August, 2017.

"Thoughts" was originally published in *Muse India*, issue 74, July-August, 2017.

"Shadow Prison" was originally published in *Muse India*, issue 74, July-August, 2017.

"Long-stalked Yellow Flower" was first published in *Erothanatos: A Peer-Reviewed Quarterly Journal on Literature*, Vol. 4, Issue 3, September, 2020.

"Places" was originally published in *Asian Signature*, April 19, 2019.

"Amphan" was originally published in *Erothanatos: A Peer-Reviewed Quarterly Journal on Literature*, Vol. 4, Issue 3, September, 2020.

"Not You Alone" was originally published in published in *Hans India*, 29th May, 2016.

Some of the poems included in this volume were previously published in *Contemporary Literary Review, Muse India, Ruminations, Kavya Bharati, East Lit. Indian Literature* (Sahitya Akademi), *Asian Signature, The Antonym, Erothanatos, Teesta Review, Setu, Poetry Potion, The Poetic Bliss* (eds. P. Gopichand and P. Nagasuseela), and *Poetry: Best of 2020* (ed D. L. Lang).

I have not included any of my poetry translations here.

About the Author

Zinia Mitra is an Associate Professor and Director of Centre for Women's Studies at the University of North Bengal. Her poems have been published in National and International journals including *Asian Signature, Contemporary Literary Review, Muse India, Ruminations, Kavya Bharati, East Lit. Indian Literature* (Sahitya Akademi), *Teesta Review, Setu, Poetry Potion, The Antonym, Erothanatos, and The Pangolin Review.*

Her translations have been published in books and journals, including *Indian Literature* (Sahitya Akademi).

Her books include *The Kali Project: Invoking the Goddess Within / Indian Women's Voices*, *Indian Poetry in English: Critical Essays*, *Poetry of Jayanta Mahapatra: Imagery and Experiential Identity*, *The Concept of Motherhood in India: Myths, Theories and Realities*, *Fourth Wave Feminism, Social Media and (Sl)Activism*. She served as the co-editor for *Twentieth Century British Literature: Reconstructing Literary Sensibility*, and *Interact*. She recently was a part of a poetry project on duoethnography under the Australian Association of Writing Program published in TEXT journal. She is on the editorial board of *Teesta Review*- an international journal of poetry.

Zinia Mitra writes from Siliguri, Darjeeling.

Another Indie Blu(e) Title You May Be Interested In:

crimson skins
Devika Mathur

Devika Mathur's haunting, visual work speaks of imagined journeys and freedoms, through imagistic and richly textured poetry. Her work challenges the accepted notions of the female, and illustrates the intensity and eloquence of her life.

https://www.amazon.com/Crimson-Skins-Devika-Mathur-ebook/dp/B08GCWK4D5

Another Indie Blu(e) Title You May Be Interested In:

As the World Burns

As the World Burns is an anthology of poetry, prose, essay, and art inspired by the unprecedented events of the year 2020. It embraces fierce and raw creative works relating to life during the Covid-19 pandemic, Black Lives Matter, Donald Trump, and the economic uncertainty and horror of the events of 2020. It is both a story of survival and an act of resistance.

https://www.amazon.com/As-World-Burns-Writers-Artists-ebook/dp/B08MYTJ5VC

Another Indie Blu(e) Title You May Be Interested In:

THE LITHIUM CHRONICLES
Nicole Lyons

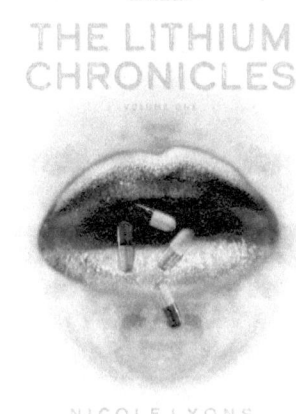

Nicole Lyons' poetry and prose are wholly relatable, taking us deep inside the heart, and the human condition. Unafraid to bare her soul, she shares her struggles skillfully crafted with every line, giving the reader permission to take a glimpse into their own.

Volume I
https://www.amazon.com/Lithium-Chronicles-One-Nicole-Lyons/dp/1732800049

Volume II
https://www.amazon.com/Lithium-Chronicles-2-Nicole-Lyons/dp/1951724011

Another Indie Blu(e) Title You May Be Interested In:

the kali project

The Kali Project draws in the voices of women as women, adding a sharper understanding of the inner realities that patriarchal structures seek to silence, sanctified by society, religion, community, and class. The gamut of experiences is vast and reiterates the idea that art and poetry are the essential vehicles which carry the hurt and, in the process, also healing within them.

https://www.amazon.com/Kali-Project-Invoking-Goddess-Within/dp/1951724062

Indie Blu(e) Publishing is a progressive, feminist micro-press, committed to producing honest and thought-provoking works. Our anthologies are meant to celebrate diversity and raise awareness. The editors all passionately advocate for human rights; mental health awareness; chronic illness awareness; sexual abuse survivors; and LGBTQ+ equality. It is our mission, and a great honor, to provide platforms for those voices that are stifled and stigmatized.

www.ingramcontent.com/pod-product-compliance
Lightning Source LLC
Chambersburg PA
CBHW022010120526
44592CB00034B/764